ORIGAMI

difficult
ORIGAMI

by Chris Alexander

Capstone
press®

Mankato, Minnesota

Snap Books are published by Capstone Press,
151 Good Counsel Drive, P.O. Box 669, Mankato, Minnesota 56002.
www.capstonepress.com

Library of Congress Cataloging-in-Publication Data
Alexander, Chris.
    Difficult origami / by Chris Alexander.
    p. cm. — (Snap books. Origami)
    Includes bibliographical references and index.
    Summary: "Provides step-by-step instructions for difficult origami models, including a cat,
a lily, a crested bird, a lop-eared rabbit, a frog, a picture frame, and a speedboat" — Provided by publisher.
    ISBN-13: 978-1-4296-2022-2 (hardcover)
    ISBN-10: 1-4296-2022-6 (hardcover)
    1. Paper work — Juvenile literature. I. Title.
TT870.A365 2009
736'.982 — dc22
                                              2007052196

Editor: Christopher L. Harbo
Designer: Bobbi J. Wyss
Photo Researcher: Dede Barton
Photo Stylist: Sarah L. Schuette
Scheduler: Marcy Morin

Photo Credits:
All principal photography in this book by Capstone Press/Karon Dubke
Capstone Press/TJ Thoraldson Digital Photography, steps (all)
William Edwards Photography, 32

1 2 3 4 5 6 13 12 11 10 09 08

page 10

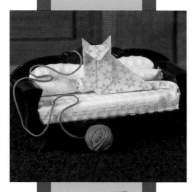

page 13

page 19

TABLE OF CONTENTS

INTRODUCTION

Welcome to the big leagues! If you've completed the projects in the first books in this series, then you're ready for a new challenge. This book will fine-tune the folding skills you've learned so far. If you've never tried origami, practice the skills in the easier books first. The models in this book have more steps, which require greater skill to complete.

So what kind of models will you find in the coming pages? You'll make a cat with a curved tail, a frog that inflates, and several other great projects. And as you master these models, experiment with them. Try making them from different types of paper. See if you can change the crested bird into a dragon. Don't be afraid to experiment with the steps. Origami is an art form. Let your inner artist shine.

MATERIALS

The color and type of paper you use plays a big part in how your models turn out. For instance, striped paper looks better on the cat than on the rabbit. And the lily looks best in a harmony paper with darker colors on its corners.

Of course, materials aren't limited to origami paper. You can use any material that holds a crease. Waterproof materials, such as foil or wax paper, might work for the boat. And construction paper will make a stronger picture frame. Experiment with materials to discover what works best for you.

HOW TO USE THIS BOOK

Origami models are made with valley folds and mountain folds. All other folds are just combinations of these two basic folds.

Valley folds are represented by a dashed line. The paper is creased along the line as the top surface of the paper is folded against itself like a book.

Mountain folds are represented by a pink dashed and dotted line. The paper is creased along the line and folded behind.

Reverse folds are made by opening a pocket slightly and folding the model inside itself along existing creases.

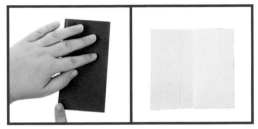

Mark folds are light folds used to make reference creases for a later step. Ideally, a mark fold will not be seen in the finished model.

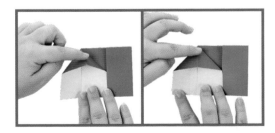

Squash folds are formed by lifting one edge of a pocket and reforming it so the spine gets flattened. The existing creases become new edges.

Outside reverse folds are two valley folds done at once. They are made by folding the model outside itself along existing creases.

Rabbit ear folds are formed by bringing two edges of a point together using existing creases. The new point is folded to one side.

FOLDING SYMBOLS

A crease from a previous step.	Fold the paper in the direction of the arrow.
A fold or edge hidden under another layer of paper; also used as an imaginary extension of an existing line.	Fold the paper and then unfold it.
Turn the paper over or rotate it to a new position.	Fold the paper behind.
Pleat the paper by reverse folding two creases.	Inflate the model by blowing air into it.

SPEEDBOAT

Traditional Model

This speedboat is a variation of an origami canoe. If you set the boat in water and blow on it, the boat will zip along nicely.

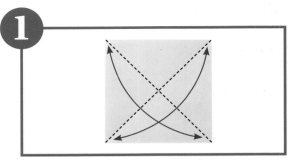

1 Start with the colored side down. Valley fold point to point in both directions and unfold.

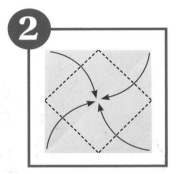

2 Valley fold the corners to the center.

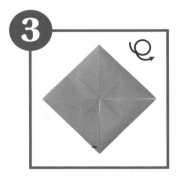

3 Turn the model over.

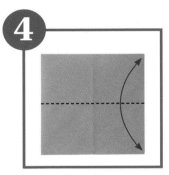

4 Valley fold in half and unfold.

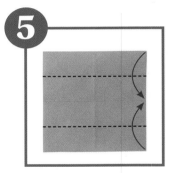

5 Valley fold the edges to the center.

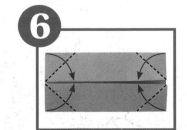

6 Valley fold the corners to the center.

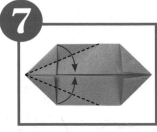

7 Valley fold to the center.

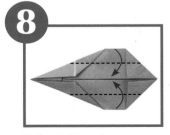

8 Valley fold to the center.

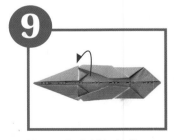

9 Mountain fold in half.

10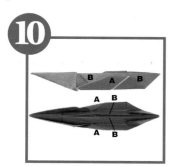

Spread the model open by holding flaps A and B together and pulling them away from the center.

11

Now push corner C inside out. Pinch the paper at D to keep it from tearing.

12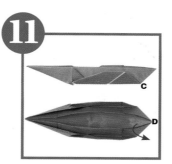

Keep pinching D while pushing the second corner inside out. Allow the hidden tail fin to pop outward.

13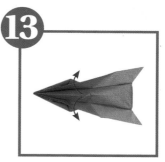

Continue rolling the sides from the back to the front until the sides are fully formed.

14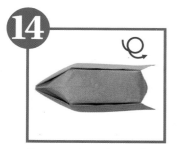

Shape and reinforce all of the creases, then turn the boat right side up.

15

Lift up the front flap.

16

Mountain fold the top third of the flap inside the model.

17

Finished speedboat.

LILY

Traditional Model

Lilies come in a variety of colors ranging from pink to black. This origami lily looks very pretty when folded with paper that has colored corners.

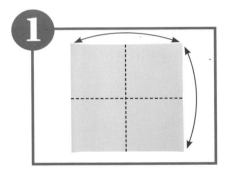

1 Start with the colored side up. Valley fold edge to edge in both directions and unfold.

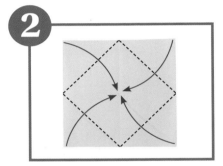

2 Valley fold the corners to the center.

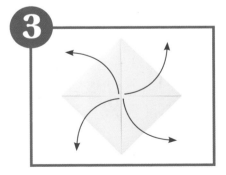

3 Unfold the corners.

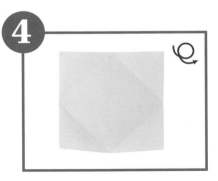

4 Turn the paper over.

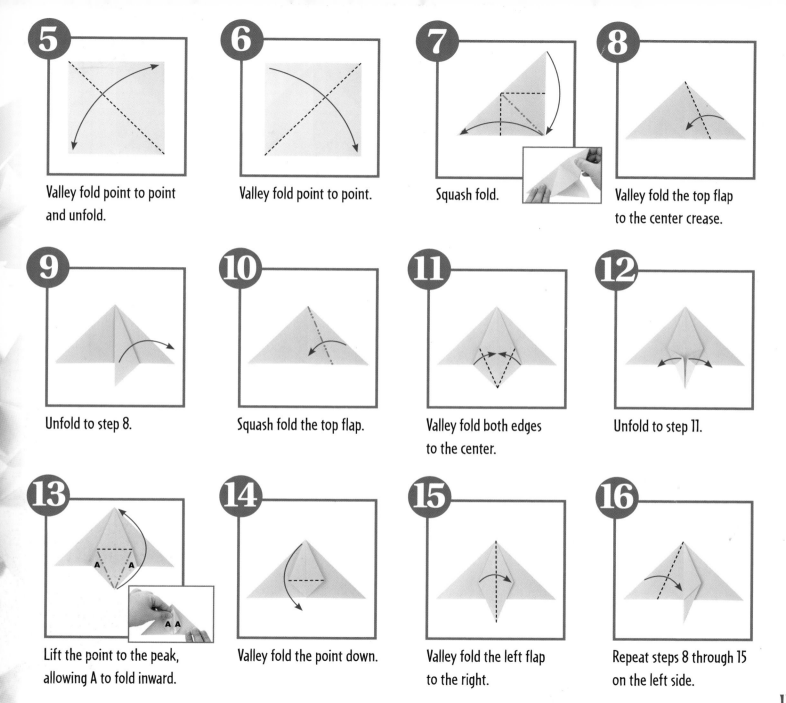

5 Valley fold point to point and unfold.

6 Valley fold point to point.

7 Squash fold.

8 Valley fold the top flap to the center crease.

9 Unfold to step 8.

10 Squash fold the top flap.

11 Valley fold both edges to the center.

12 Unfold to step 11.

13 Lift the point to the peak, allowing A to fold inward.

14 Valley fold the point down.

15 Valley fold the left flap to the right.

16 Repeat steps 8 through 15 on the left side.

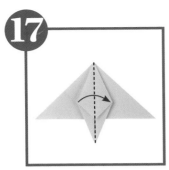

17

Valley fold the left side to the right.

18

Turn the model over.

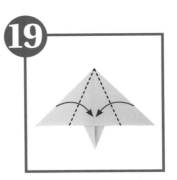

19

Repeat steps 8 through 17 on this side.

20

Rotate the model so the four points are on top.

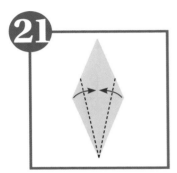

21

Valley fold the top flaps to the center.

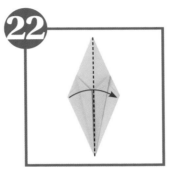

22

Valley fold the top two flaps to the right.

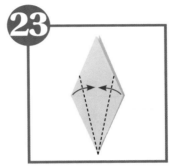

23

Repeat step 21 on this side.

24

Turn the model over.

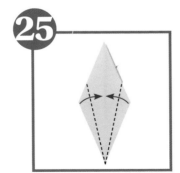

25

Repeat steps 21 through 23 on this side.

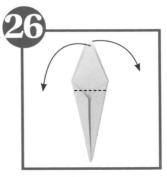

26

Valley fold the top petal halfway down. Repeat on the back petal.

27

Valley fold the remaining two petals halfway down.

28

Finished lily.

CATNIP THE CAT

Model designed by Chris Alexander

The ancient Egyptians believed cats were living gods. Judging by their attitudes, most cats still feel this way today. An extremely proud cat named Catnip inspired this model.

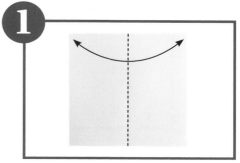

1 Start with the colored side down. Valley fold in half and unfold.

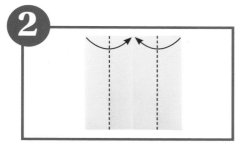

2 Valley fold the edges to the center.

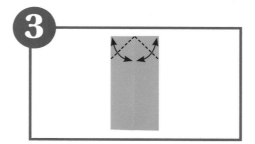

3 Valley fold the corners to the center and unfold.

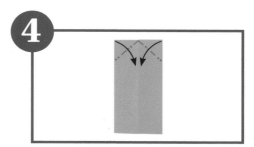

4 Reverse fold on the creases formed in step 3.

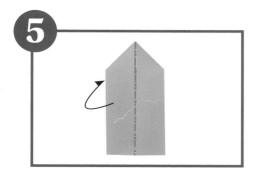

5 Mountain fold the left side behind the right side.

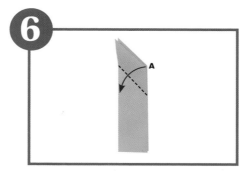

6 Valley fold corner A to the edge.

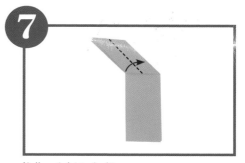

7 Valley fold in half.

13

8

Unfold the crease formed in step 6, then turn the model over.

9

Unfold the top layer to the left and squash fold the hidden triangle.

10

Mountain fold, forming a right angle at the corner. Turn the model over.

11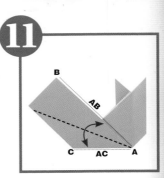

Valley fold edge AB even with edge AC and unfold.

12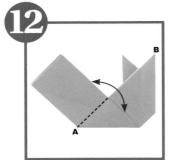

Valley fold even with edge AB and unfold.

13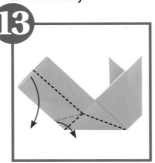

Rabbit ear fold on the creases made in steps 11 and 12.

14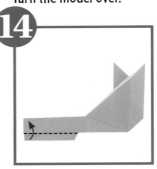

Valley fold the exposed section of the tail.

15

Valley fold the tail in half.

16

Valley fold the ear down even with the top of the head.

17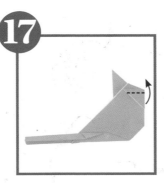

Valley fold about ¾ of the way back up.

18

Unfold to step 16.

19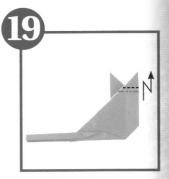

Pleat fold on the creases formed in steps 16 and 17.

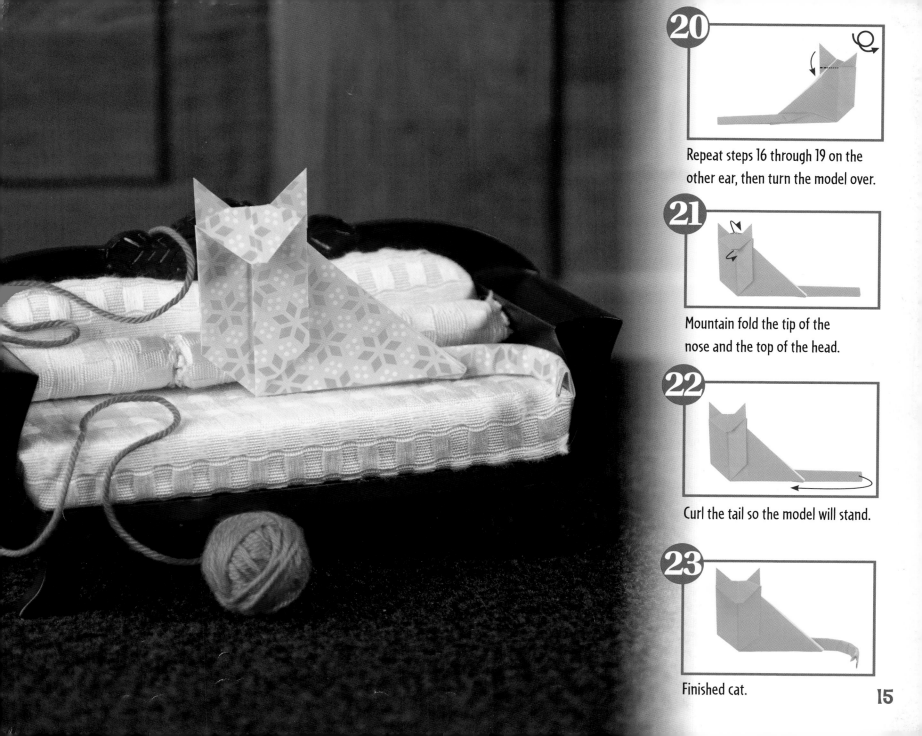

20

Repeat steps 16 through 19 on the other ear, then turn the model over.

21

Mountain fold the tip of the nose and the top of the head.

22

Curl the tail so the model will stand.

23

Finished cat.

15

PICTURE FRAME

Model designed by Chris Alexander

This three-dimensional frame will highlight almost any size picture. Start with a square sheet of paper at least 50 percent larger than the long side of the picture.

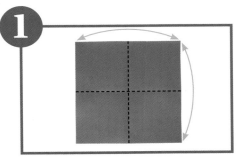

1

Start with the colored side up. Mark fold from edge to edge in both directions and unfold.

2

Using the creases for alignment, center the picture on the paper.

3

Valley fold even with the edge of the picture and unfold.

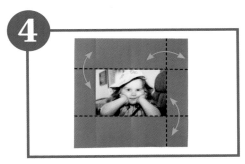

4

Valley fold and unfold the other three sides.

5

Remove the picture and turn the paper over.

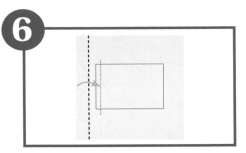

6

Valley fold the paper about ¼ of an inch over the crease.

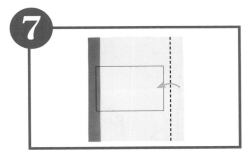

7

Valley fold the paper about ¼ of an inch over the crease.

8

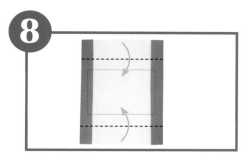

Valley fold the paper about ¼ of an inch over the crease.

9

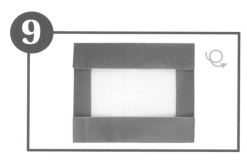

Turn the paper over.

10

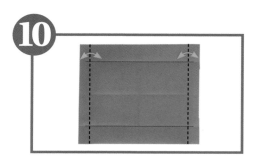

Valley fold on the creases formed in steps 3 and 4 and unfold.

11

Valley fold on the creases formed in step 4 and unfold.

12

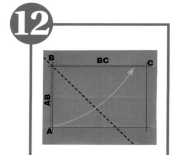

Valley fold crease AB even with crease BC.

13

Unfold.

14

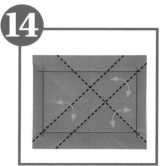

Repeat steps 12 and 13 on the other three corners.

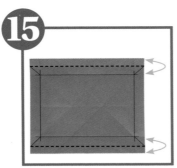

15

Valley fold even with the ends of the creases formed in steps 12 and 14 and unfold.

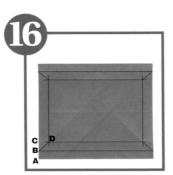

16

If the distance between A and B is smaller than between C and D, skip to step 18.

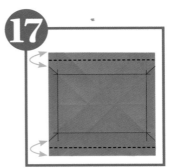

17

Valley fold only if AB was larger than CD in step 16.

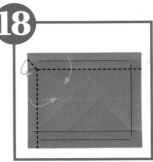

18

Rabbit ear fold to form a boxlike corner.

19

Valley fold the extended flap even with the back side of the box.

20

Repeat steps 16 through 19 on the other three corners.

21

Unfold the model completely. Place the picture inside and refold everything up to this step.

22

Valley fold on the crease formed in step 15.

23

Repeat step 22 on this side.

24

Stand up the frame.

25

Finished picture frame.

LOP-EARED RABBIT

Model designed by Chris Alexander

Lop-eared rabbits have long, floppy ears that hang down and touch the ground. This unique feature gives this model a comic personality.

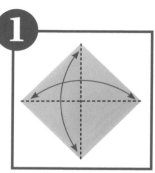

1 Start with the colored side up. Valley fold point to point in both directions and unfold.

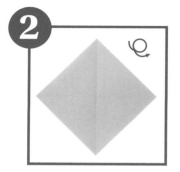

2 Turn the paper over.

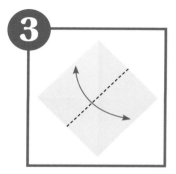

3 Valley fold edge to edge and unfold.

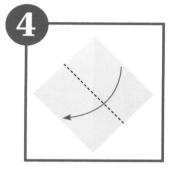

4 Valley fold edge to edge.

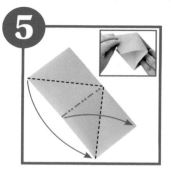

5 Squash fold.

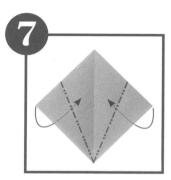

6 Valley fold the top flaps to the center and unfold. Repeat behind.

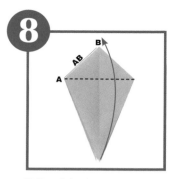

7 Reverse fold the flaps. Repeat behind.

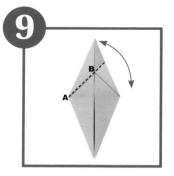

8 Valley fold. Note edge AB for step 9.

9 Valley fold the left side on the hidden edge and unfold. Repeat on right side.

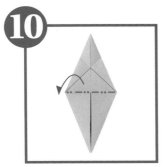

10 Mountain fold the triangle in the back all the way down.

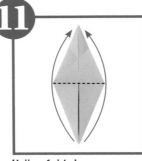

11 Valley fold the two points up.

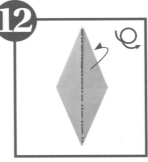

12 Mountain fold and rotate the model.

13 Valley fold the top flap even with the crease formed in step 9. Repeat behind.

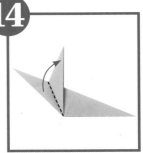

14 Valley fold even with the crease formed in step 13.

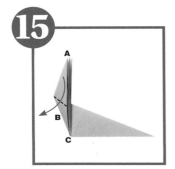

15 Valley fold so A, B, and C form a right angle.

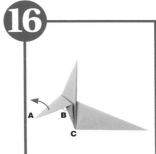

16 Unfold to step 14.

17 Squash fold on the creases formed in steps 14 and 15.

18 Valley fold the point so it almost reaches the corner.

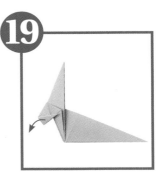

19 Unfold the point.

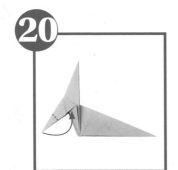

20 Reverse fold on the crease formed in step 18.

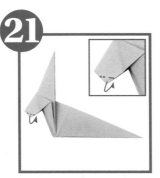

21 Mountain fold into the head. Repeat behind.

22 Valley fold the ear. Repeat behind.

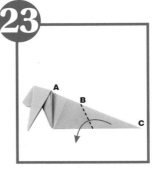

23 Valley fold so A, B, and C form a right angle.

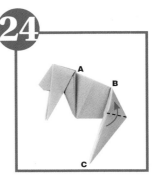

24 Valley fold even with edge CB.

25

Valley fold even with the edge formed in step 23.

26

Valley fold even with the edge formed in step 24.

27

Unfold to step 23.

28

Reverse fold on the creases formed in steps 23 and 24.

29

Squash fold on the creases formed in steps 25 and 26.

30

Valley fold in half and unfold.

31

Reverse fold on the crease formed in step 30.

32

Tuck flap A inside the back of the body. Repeat behind.

33

Finished lop-eared rabbit.

CRESTED BIRD

Model designed by Chris Alexander

The unique feature of this bird is a feather crest on the top of its head. This basic bird model represents crested birds such as the long-crested eagle or the crested goshawk.

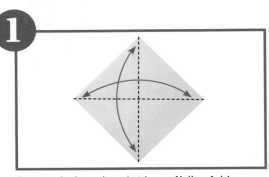

1

Start with the colored side up. Valley fold point to point in both directions and unfold.

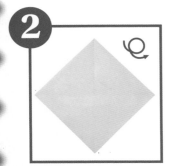

2

Turn the paper over.

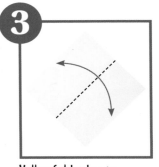

3

Valley fold edge to edge and unfold.

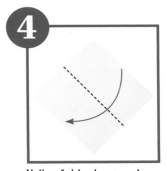

4

Valley fold edge to edge.

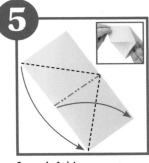

5

Squash fold.

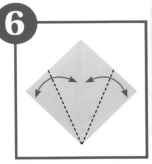

6

Valley fold the top flaps to the center and unfold. Repeat behind.

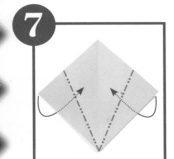

7

Reverse fold the flaps. Repeat behind.

8

Valley fold the top flap to the center and unfold.

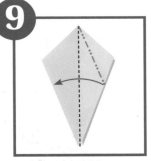

9

Squash fold on the crease formed in step 8.

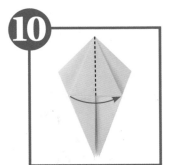

10

Valley fold the top flap to the right side.

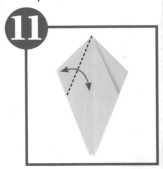

11

Repeat steps 8 through 10 on the left side.

12

Turn the model over.

13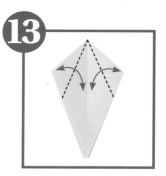

Repeat steps 8 through 11 on this side.

14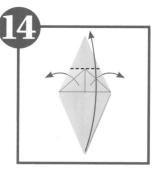

Valley fold the top flap up as far as it will go. Allow the hidden triangles to unfold.

15

Valley fold the top flaps.

16

Unfold the flaps.

17

Reverse fold the top flaps on the creases formed in step 15.

18

Valley fold. The creases go from point to corner and do not meet in the center.

19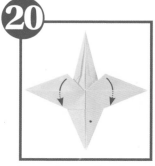

Unfold the top flaps.

20

Insert the top flaps into the pockets of the bottom flaps.

23

21

Valley fold the point to the edge of the wings and unfold.

22

Spread the edges apart and valley fold the tip inside the opening.

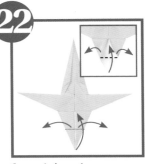

23

Valley fold the edges outward.

24

Valley fold the point down. The crease starts where the edges meet.

25

Valley fold even with the edge of the wings.

26

Valley fold the head down. Start the crease just above the crease formed in step 25.

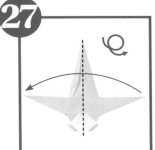

27

Valley fold in half and rotate the model.

28

Gently pivot the head down.

29

Outside reverse fold to form the legs. There are no guide marks for this step.

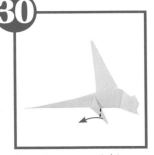

30

Outside reverse fold to form the feet. There are no guide marks for this step.

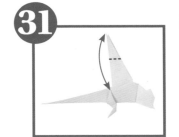

31

Valley fold the tip of the wing to the top of the leg and unfold. Repeat behind.

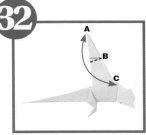

32

Valley fold so edge AB lays on edge BC and unfold. Repeat behind.

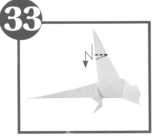

33

Pleat fold on the creases formed in steps 31 and 32. Repeat behind.

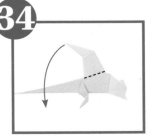

34

Valley fold the wing down. Repeat behind.

35

Finished crested bird.

CLASSIC FROG

Traditional Model

Frogs have inspired many origami models. This version is fun because you inflate the frog when you're done folding. Just try not to laugh when you blow air into its rear end.

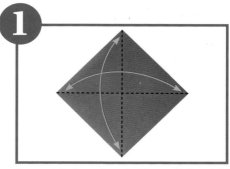

1 Start with the colored side up. Valley fold point to point in both directions and unfold.

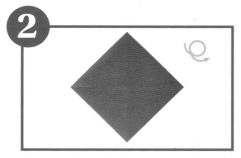

2 Turn the paper over.

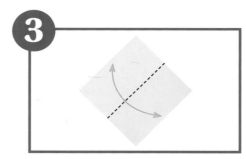

3 Valley fold edge to edge and unfold.

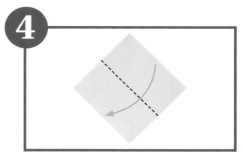

4 Valley fold edge to edge.

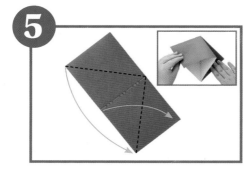

5 Squash fold.

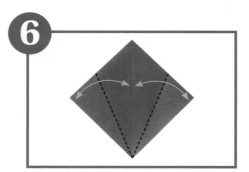

6 Valley fold the top flaps to the center and unfold. Repeat behind.

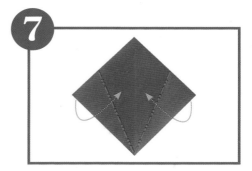

7 Reverse fold the flaps. Repeat behind.

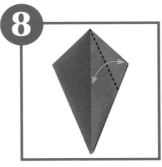

8

Valley fold the top flap to the center and unfold.

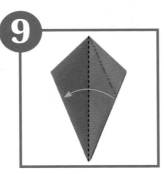

9

Squash fold on the crease formed in step 8.

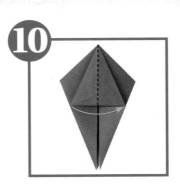

10

Valley fold the top flap to the right side.

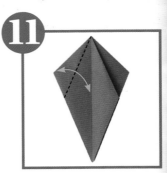

11

Repeat steps 8 through 10 on the left side.

12

Turn the model over.

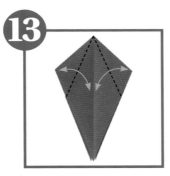

13

Repeat steps 8 through 11 on this side.

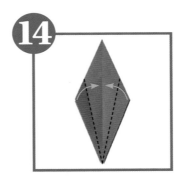

14

Valley fold the top flaps to the center.

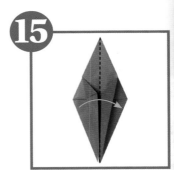

15

Valley fold the top two flaps to the right side.

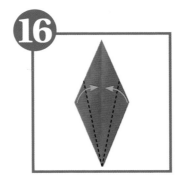

16

Repeat steps 14 through 15 on this side.

17

Turn the model over.

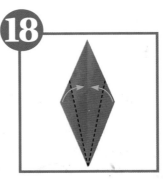

18

Repeat steps 14 through 16 on this side.

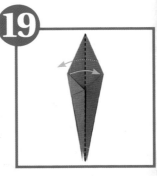

19

Valley fold the top flap to the right and the back flap to the left.

20

Valley fold the top flap
so it lays on edge AB.

21

Unfold the flap.

22

Reverse fold on the crease
formed in step 20.

23

Repeat steps 20 through
22 on the top right flap.

27

24 Reverse fold the bottom leg almost straight out. There are no guide marks for this step.

25 Reverse fold the other leg to about the same position.

26 Valley fold the legs about 1/3 of the way from the body. There are no guides for this step.

27 Valley fold the legs at the halfway point. There are no guides for this step.

28 Unfold to step 26.

29 Reverse fold on the creases formed in step 26.

30 Reverse fold on the creases formed in step 27.

31 Unfold the bottom half of the feet.

32 Mountain fold the front legs down, starting just outside of the body.

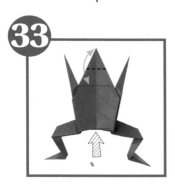

33 Valley fold and unfold. Then gently inflate the body.

34 Mountain fold the two points to form the front feet.

35 Finished frog.

FUN FACTS

A custom is centered on the origami crane. It says if you think about a wish while making 1,000 cranes, your wish will come true.

The paper crane is also a symbol of peace. In December 2004, the government of Thailand used planes to drop 100 million paper cranes over southern Thailand. The cranes were dropped in an effort to restore peace to the people fighting there.

The origins of origami can be traced back to Japan about 1,500 years ago. But the art of folding paper also developed in other parts of the world. In fact, people called the Moors introduced paper folding to the Spanish about 900 years ago.

The Secret of One Thousand Cranes Origami is the oldest known origami book. This book was published in 1797.

The longest modular origami model was a gum wrapper chain created by Gary Duschl. The chain measured more than 9 miles (14 kilometers). It used more than 1 million gum wrappers.

Every year, the American Museum of Natural History in New York City decorates an origami holiday tree. The tree stands 19 feet (5.8 meters) tall. It holds hundreds of origami models folded by members of OrigamiUSA. This organization promotes the art of paper folding in the United States.

GLOSSARY

align (uh-LINE) — to put a series of things in a straight line

attitude (AT-i-tood) — your opinions or feelings about someone or something

crease (KREES) — to make lines or folds in something

crest (KREST) — a comb or tuft of feathers on a bird's head

inflate (in-FLATE) — to make something expand by blowing or pumping air into it

modular (MAH-juh-luhr) — made up of several separate pieces or sections

reinforce (ree-in-FORSS) — to strengthen the structure or shape of something

reverse (ri-VURSS) — opposite in position, order, or direction

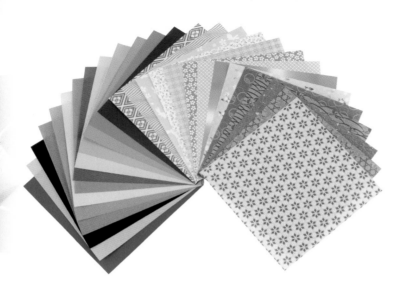

READ MORE

Alexander, Chris. *Sort-of-Difficult Origami.* Origami. Mankato, Minn.: Capstone Press, 2009.

Gross, Gay Merrill. *Minigami: Mini Origami Projects for Cards, Gifts, and Decorations.* Richmond Hill, Ont.: Firefly Books, 2005.

Montroll, John. *Dollar Bill Origami.* Mineola, N.Y.: Dover, 2003.

INTERNET SITES

FactHound offers a safe, fun way to find Internet sites related to this book. All of the sites on FactHound have been researched by our staff.

Here's how:
1. Visit *www.facthound.com*
2. Choose your grade level.
3. Type in this book ID **1429620226** for age-appropriate sites. You may also browse subjects by clicking on letters, or by clicking on pictures and words.
4. Click on the **Fetch It** button.

FactHound will fetch the best sites for you!

ABOUT THE AUTHOR

Chris Alexander was born and raised in New York City. At the age of 5, he had his first experience with origami. During a visit to the public library, he came across a book with simple folding instructions. After successfully completing a paper cup, he was instantly hooked on the art. He insisted upon using the flimsy cup at dinner, but his mother urged him to learn other models instead. Almost 40 years and a multitude of "other models" later, Chris has created approximately 100 original models. Directions for some of them are found in this book.

INDEX